D0318919

TAEKWONDO

THE COMPLETE COURSE

JOHN GOLDMAN
BLACK BELT 5th DAN

GUINNESS PUBLISHING

DEDICATION
To those who enjoy Taekwondo, with or without ambition

Editor: Charles Richards
Text design and layout: Amanda Sedge
Photography by John Gichigi

Copyright © John Goldman 1991

The right of John Goldman to be identified as the Author of this Work has been asserted in accordance with the Copyright, Design & Patents Act 1988.

Published in Great Britain by Guinness Publishing Ltd, 33 London Road, Enfield, Middlesex

All rights reserved. No part of this publication may be reproduced, stored in a retrieval system, or transmitted in any form or by any means, electronic, mechanical, photocopying, recording or otherwise without prior permission in writing of the publisher.

Typeset in Gill Sans by Ace Filmsetting Ltd, Frome, Somerset
Printed and bound in Great Britain by The Bath Press, Bath, Avon

'Guinness' is a registered trademark of Guinness Publishing Ltd

British Library Cataloguing in Publication Data
Goldman, John
   Taekwondo; the complete course
   1. Taekwondo
   1. Title
   796.815

ISBN 0-85112-950-1

THE AUTHOR

John Goldman has been active in the martial arts for twenty years; for the past eight as a full-time instructor. His involvement in recent years in self-defence led him to an appreciation of the growing popularity of Taekwondo.

John has travelled to many parts of the world studying the martial arts – to Canada, the United States, Spain and Japan, where he was the guest of the world-renowned Budo master, the late Kenshiro Abbe.

In 1980 John constructed one of Britain's first purpose-built martial arts halls (*dojangs*) in the West Country, and he still teaches there today. His teaching experience has been wide; his students include police, deaf children and women's groups.

Apart from his teaching he organises national conventions and competitions for Taekwondo and other martial arts. This is his third book for Guinness; the others are *Judo; The Complete Course* and *Self-defence; The Complete Course*.

CONTENTS

FOREWORD 5

1 HOW IT BEGAN 7

2 IS IT FOR ME? 8

3 FINDING A GOOD CLUB 9

4 BOWING – IS IT NECESSARY? . 10

5 COURTESY, COURAGE
AND CONTROL 11

6 GETTING KITTED OUT 12

7 TAKING CARE 14

8 FROM WHITE TO BLACK 15

9 TECHNIQUES IN ACTION 17

　　Destruction 17

　　Self-defence 18

　　Sparring 19

　　Competition 19

　　Patterns 20

10 GETTING INTO SHAPE 24

　　Loosening up 24

　　Warming up 26

　　Stretching 28

　　Isometrics 32

11 STRIKING OUT 35

　　Targets 35

　　Weapons 36

12 AT THE READY 41

13 COMING TO BLOWS 45

　　The making of a fist 45

　　Punching 46

　　Hand weapons on target 48

　　Kicking 53

14 ON GUARD 67

15 SET YOUR SIGHTS 78

16 SPARRING 83

　　Three-step sparring 83

　　Two-step sparring 92

　　One-step sparring 104

　　Free sparring 119

17 COMPETITION 121

18 DESTRUCTION 124

19 SELF-DEFENCE 128

20 JO'S STORY 141

21 PATTERNS 142

　ACKNOWLEDGEMENTS 160

　USEFUL ADDRESSES 160

FOREWORD

We practitioners of Taekwondo, a rapidly expanding martial art, are so busy training and competing that we have little time for writing. John Goldman, happily, is a natural writer as well as being a thoroughly experienced martial artist with twenty years' devotion behind him.

His book, *Taekwondo; The Complete Course*, is his third. It is understandable that he now has a large following, for his style is relaxed and entertaining as well as being spot-on for accuracy and professionalism.

Many authors tell the reader what they want to tell them; John's objective approach throughout the book tells the student what he needs to know. From finding a good club to performing a pattern for Black Belt examinations, *Taekwondo; The Complete Course* says it all clearly, missing nothing of vital importance to the serious student.

Whatever your style, whatever your level, I can thoroughly recommend this book.

DAVE OLIVER 5th DAN

Dave Oliver is a Black Belt 5th Dan, International Taekwondo Federation and World Taekwondo Federation. He is the public relations officer for the British Taekwondo Council – the governing body of Taekwondo in Great Britain – and also Chairman of the Taekwondo Association of Great Britain.

A former British champion and international, Dave coached the British team to win the 1981 ITF world championships in Argentina and the world open championships in Leicester in 1988. That same year he was voted foreign instructor of the year by the American magazine Taekwondo Times.

HOW IT BEGAN

Taekwondo is the Korean name for the 'Art of foot and hand fighting'. There is no other martial art style like it. Jumping and spinning in the air and striking out with hands and feet are its special characteristics. These can be spectacular. Throughout the world there are many styles of foot and hand fighting but none is so enjoyable in its freedom of expression.

The history of the martial arts is steeped in romanticism and there are many theories concerning its origins. China, Japan, Korea and India all have strong claims to the beginnings of unarmed combat, while fighting skills were a natural development throughout the world for self-protection.

Korean martial arts began more than two thousand years ago. In 1955 a special board was formed to name and control a nationally recognised and authoritative art that could be taught to the people and the military. Martial arts masters, politicians, historians and leading members of society pooled their ideas and expertise. It was a member of that group, Major-General Choi Hong Hi, who gave this new art the name Taekwondo. Today there are more than twenty million practitioners of Taekwondo worldwide. It was introduced as a demonstration sport at the 1988 Seoul Olympics.

In 1967 Master Rhee Ki Ha promoted Taekwondo in Great Britain. There are now more than forty thousand men, women, boys and girls practising in this country. A number of associations have been formed to give their membership support, advice and training, and to arrange competitions. These associations come under the umbrella of the British Taekwondo Council. Membership of Taekwondo is growing week by week as new clubs open up in sports halls, YMCAs and other centres. Taekwondo is an exercise, an art, a form of self-defence, a discipline and a sport. Anyone can take part.

The leap is mightier than the sword.

2

IS IT FOR ME?

The opening ceremony at the 1988 Olympics in Seoul. More than one thousand Taekwondo Black Belt experts took part!

When I began to study the martial arts , I looked for an enjoyable, physical form of recreation with the added benefit of self-defence. I never really enjoyed team games at school but what I found myself doing in football, rugby and basketball, was to single out an opponent and pit my wits and skill against his. It's the one-to-one combat situation that attracts many people to Taekwondo and the other martial arts.

However, people take up Taekwondo for a variety of reasons. Some join to boost their self-confidence, others to master self-defence. You may see the prospect of entering competitions as exciting; or aspire to the grace and beauty of body movement. You may want to be a Black Belt; there is a progressive examination structure (grading) in which you are awarded coloured belts on the way to the coveted 'black'.

For some the fascination of learning techniques and performing them to exacting standards may be the attraction. Others enjoy being part of a disciplined group of people from all walks of life, of all ages and both sexes, who can work together and help fulfil their aims. It is not unusual to find a 12-year-old or a 70-year-old sporting a Black Belt. You may simply want to get fit or improve your flexibility; or, like me, you may (initially anyway) just want a physical form of recreation.

As you will quickly recognise, there is a host of personal benefits to be gained from regular training. Taekwondo is a way of disciplining yourself and finding new goals. You may never have considered becoming a Black Belt but now you strive to do so. You may have been attracted to the competitive side of the art but did not know how unfit you really were. Now you are determined to work hard at becoming really fit. On the other hand you may have a super-fit body and not know what use to put it to.

You are never at a dead end. Taekwondo exercises are very different from the familiar sit-ups and press-ups. The stretching exercises you will learn will shape you up for a new range of activities. Whatever your reason for starting, Taekwondo will have a lot more to offer than you originally thought.

FINDING A GOOD CLUB

3

Taekwondo is first and foremost a martial art to be practised with control. Sloppy practice or fooling around can lead to injury. Strict rules of conduct and close attention to them will ensure that injuries are kept to a minimum.

There are no actual laws to govern Taekwondo clubs but each organisation under the British Taekwondo Council strives to maintain the highest standards. If there are several clubs (*dojangs*) in your area, visit all of them. Talk to the instructors – they should be pleased to have you watching a class.

If you have visited a traditional Karate class and found it rather too formal or regimented, you will recognise that Taekwondo is more modern in its approach. None of the etiquette or discipline has been overlooked but there is an air of enjoyment.

Many Karate exponents are now training in Taekwondo as it is in many ways more progressive, more dynamic, more exciting and more entertaining.

In a good club there should be a feeling of friendliness. The pace may be fast and training may be tough at times but nobody should be getting hurt. If the club has been going for a few years there should be, apart from the instructor, some other high grades, Blue, Red and Black Belts, practising. If there are not, then it may be that they are leaving before progressing up the ladder. Find out why.

Getting to know each other – and a few techniques.

4

BOWING – IS IT NECESSARY?

A boy of 13 once came to my class to watch. I asked him what he thought of it.

'Good!' he said. 'But I can't join; my parents won't let me.'

'Why?' I asked.

'Because it's religious,' came the reply. I was naturally surprised until he explained that it was 'all this bowing'.

The simple act of bowing on entering the *dojang* is your commitment to conducting yourself in a proper manner during training. You also bow as you leave the class. This does not mean that you then go home and conduct yourself in an unacceptable way! Training in the martial arts and observing codes of discipline and etiquette help to instil a good attitude in or out of class.

During training there should be no idle chatter, running around or fooling about. You are part of a group, each member of which is intent on making progress. Bowing to a partner before and after practice is a sign of respect. Even in the heat of competition you have a responsibility. You want to win and must fight to do so. However, there is no room for bad temper.

At the start of a class the students form a line in front of the instructor. A mark of mutual respect is again made by bowing. The class can then begin with everyone in the right frame of mind. The class will also end with the formal bow. This is a way of saying thank you – the student to the instructor, the instructor to the student.

Bowing – it embodies respect and courtesy.

COURTESY, COURAGE AND CONTROL

5

The *do* in Taekwondo, as in the other martial arts of Judo and Aikido, means 'a way'. A way of doing things that will bring you benefit. This 'way' is not only for the development of the body; it stimulates the mind as well. Doing something well can make you feel good. Doing things correctly with control and an understanding of personal welfare and respect for others can help to encourage self-discipline, humility, confidence, self-awareness and many other qualities.

The tenets of Taekwondo are:

COURTESY To be polite to one's instructors, seniors and fellow students.

INTEGRITY To be honest with one's self. One must be able to define right and wrong.

PERSEVERANCE To achieve a goal, whether it is a higher grade or technique, you must not stop trying; you must persevere.

SELF-CONTROL To lose one's temper when performing techniques against an opponent can be dangerous and shows lack of self-control. To be able to live, work and train within one's capability shows good self-control.

INDOMITABLE SPIRIT To show courage; even when you and your principles are pitted against overwhelming odds.

6   GETTING KITTED OUT

TAEKWONDO THE COMPLETE COURSE

Now you've decided to give it a go, it won't be long before you're hooked. The next step is to get yourself kitted out in a Taekwondo suit, a *dobok*. You'll feel good when you put this on for the first time, a member of the group, ready for action. The best place to buy your uniform is from your own club. The suits are made from cotton, are comfortable to wear and easy to look after. They should be kept clean, pressed and in good repair.

It's a good idea at a later date to buy a tracksuit. This can be worn over the Taekwondo uniform and will keep you warm during intervals in training or competition. A tracksuit will also cover your uniform on your journey to the club. It is not a good idea to walk around advertising the fact that you do Taekwondo. You don't want to be a show-off.

Your uniform comes complete with a white belt. This is the belt you wear until you progress through to the next colour after passing the grading examination.

Facing page: Our models kitted out in style. Martin (left) is a Black Belt 2nd Dan and so is his daughter Jo. Both are wearing International Taekwondo Federation (ITF) uniforms. Roger, a Black Belt 1st Dan, wears the World Taekwondo Federation (WTF) outfit. You'll see a lot more of these three throughout the book.

William and his sister Clauda are in combat gear. William's chest protector is compulsory for **WTF** full contact competitions. Competitors in ITF semi-contact bouts wear hand and foot protectors, as Clauda shows.

7 TAKING CARE

Safety procedures are a priority in all martial arts. So is hygiene. You must pay attention to personal cleanliness.

You will look smart in your new, neatly pressed uniform. Don't spoil it all by turning up for class with dirty hands or feet. Keep finger and toenails short – long nails can cause injury while a torn nail will cause you pain.

Remove all hard and sharp objects such as rings or necklaces. Tie long hair back – you want to see what you're doing!

All students have a duty to the other members of the club. They must follow simple rules to make Taekwondo a safe and enjoyable sport.

'Honest, my hands and feet are clean!' – action from the 1985 World Games.

FROM WHITE TO BLACK

8

After three or four months' training you will be ready to enter your first grading examination. On joining the club you will have been shown a syllabus by your instructor. You will be able to purchase a syllabus; it details what you need to do for each examination as you progress through the coloured belts.

Everyone gets nervous at gradings; so don't worry, the examiners will understand. There may be two or three examiners forming a panel. They will ask you to do some of the moves that you have been practising in class. Take your time – there is no hurry. If you make a mistake, try to correct it by doing the move again. If you practise twice weekly at your club and go through moves by yourself in your spare time at home, it won't be long before you are able to do competently what you have been shown. It is only through

The belt is wrapped once round the body so that both ends come to the front.

Cross one end over the other . . .

. . . tuck the top end under the belt and draw it out again in front.

Tie a reef-knot with the two ends.

your own efforts and diligent and continuous practice that you will improve. There is no reason why anyone should not be an expert in their chosen art.

Gradings are normally held every three to four months and if you have been practising regularly twice a week for this period, you should be ready to enter. There are ten grades (*kups*) before you reach Black Belt. On attaining Black Belt 1st Degree you will have to train for 18 months before applying to enter another examination for Black Belt 2nd Degree. Whatever your level, there is always something new to learn and the need to perfect what you already know.

The colour of the belt to wear at each grade level is:

10th Kup	White belt
9th	White with yellow tab
8th	Yellow belt
7th	Yellow with green tab
6th	Green belt
5th	Green with blue tab
4th	Blue belt
3rd	Blue with red tab
2nd	Red belt
1st	Red with black tab
1st Dan	Black Belt

TECHNIQUES IN ACTION

9

Taekwondo offers you variety. You may decide at a later date to specialise in one particular area of training.

DESTRUCTION

Breaking a piece of wood in two is not a macho feat. This kind of demonstration in Taekwondo is to show the effectiveness of certain techniques.

Martial arts came about from a need for self-defence. Today's martial arts still offer their practitioners methods of defence and attack that could be fully effective in the face of danger. If these arts were to be merely for sport there would be no need to demonstrate their effectiveness as a form of defence and in fact they would probably become less useful. Taekwondo is taught with defence in mind.

Martin demonstrates the force of a knife hand strike. Splitting timber two inches thick is a routine exercise for Martin; it is not for the novice. Highly-trained Black Belts can break thick blocks of concrete.

Martin's yell is not mere play-acting; it's an essential part of the build-up of energy.

Children are not allowed to practise destructive feats such as breaking wood. Adults are not shown any of these techniques until they have practised Taekwondo for some time. Even then they will practise on the thinnest of boards and under strict supervision.

The class practise a simple but effective move – a palm heel strike to the chin.

SELF-DEFENCE

All the techniques you see in this book, and those you are taught in the classroom, are potentially dangerous. They would all, if executed with full force, cause severe injury to an unprotected opponent. Always remember that the techniques you perform, whether in class, sparring or competition, are governed by rules.

A fancy move you do in the club in response to the actions of another trained martial artist may fail miserably against an assailant in the street. Simple moves, such as a low kick, are more effective.

If you are attacked, you have every right to defend yourself but legally you may only use as much force as is reasonably necessary to ward off an attacker.

SPARRING

Sparring allows the Taekwondo student to become involved in the excitement of the sport at a very early stage in training. In a safe but challenging way, two students can practise with each other.

To begin, one attacks. The other defends and then responds by striking back. All these moves, at this stage anyway, are planned beforehand. As you become more experienced the sparring is freer and you need to be more alert.

Clauda moves smartly away from Jo's attack. Both girls are kitted out in safety gear – just in case!

Sparring teaches distancing, timing, and controlled contact. It is a demanding form of exercise and will certainly increase your fitness. We'll deal more with sparring after you have learned some of the basic Taekwondo techniques.

COMPETITION

If you want to take part in competition you need to be fit. Competition is not an excuse for going wild, and bad temper plays no part in the sport. Fighting spirit and controlled actions are the hallmarks of a good competitor.

There are two forms of competition, both very demanding. One is semi-contact (ITF), the other is full contact (WTF). It is the full contact system which has been adopted as an Olympic sport. To take part in competition at this level you will first have to achieve Black Belt!

The rules of competition are strict, always controlled by qualified referees. In a later chapter you will learn about them.

Taekwondo at the 1988 Olympics in Seoul.

PATTERNS

A pattern is performed as an individual exercise. It is a series of movements and techniques put together in a pre-arranged sequence. Judo and Karate also have patterns which are an integral part of training. They represent combat situations: defence and attacks against an imaginary opponent or opponents.

Training in patterns increases your skill and powers of concentration. Repeated practice helps you in time to respond automatically to an attack whether in sparring, competition or in the face of real danger. It is through these patterns that the martial artist strives for perfection.

Martin demonstrates here the opening moves of a basic pattern.

From a ready stance Martin . . .

. . . turns and prepares to block . . .

. . . with his left arm.

He steps forward and punches.

He then prepares to block an attack from behind . . .

. . . with his right arm.

Stepping forward, he follows up with a punch.

The pattern is continued with Martin making several more moves and turns. This sequence ends (as do all patterns) with Martin back in the same position and at the same spot at which he started.

10

GETTING INTO SHAPE

For any physical activity, preparation is essential. Taekwondo is a strenuous sport. If your body is not properly loosened up before practice you're asking for trouble.

A car's engine needs warming up before you start off in the morning. So does your body. Trying to get away quickly in top gear won't do the car any good and it certainly won't do you any good – you might find yourself in for repair!

However, with your muscles pumping and joints flexing, you'll be surprised how much extra strength and speed you put into training.

Fitness training in Taekwondo is not just for strength and stamina. Flexibility plays a key role. Particular attention is paid to the hips, which give the kicking techniques their power.

You will be introduced to a new range of exercises to increase suppleness. Stretching and arching movements are a vital part of the warm-up period at the start of each class. But remember, go easy. It's your body and you want to improve its functions.

You're bound to ache a little, as you'll be using muscles that have not been tested for a while. You may be a bit stiff the first few mornings after a class but this will soon wear off. Once you know your body, you can begin to challenge yourself, push a little, stretch another inch. Exercise is a serious and necessary part of training and it will bring real benefit. You'll surprise yourself.

The following are exercises from one of the many varied warm-up programmes you will learn in class. Don't wait for the next lesson to do them again, do them every day!

LOOSENING UP

Gently does it. Exercises are designed to do different jobs but none should be done vigorously at first. Get the circulation going and joints moving.

Loosening up the neck.

Expanding the chest by pulling back the shoulders.

Rotating the knees – don't forget the hips and ankles.

This flexes the spine – keep your chin tucked in.

WARMING UP

Now the real work starts. You've loosened up and now you're warming up.

Sit up and twist.

Press-ups with a difference – Roger has to push up against Jo's weight. Don't forget to change over!

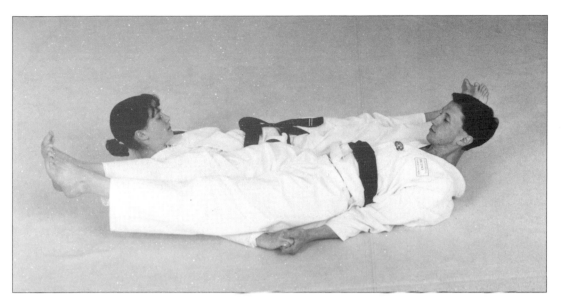

Head to toe, clasp hands, and note that feet are off the ground. Now . . .

. . . lift hips and swing legs across to come down on the other side. Keep going from side to side but watch those feet, make sure they don't touch the floor.

Begin at a comfortable height, making sure the leg is straight.

STRETCHING

Now it's time to stretch. A partner comes in handy here too.

It's that little bit extra each time that makes the difference.

Another good way – Jo has now come forward to use the weight of her body as extra pressure.

Stretching is vital to Taekwondo. High kicks come only with persistent exercising and flexibility of the hip is the key. Effective punching and kicking techniques rely heavily on the swivel-power of the hip.

On the next few pages are some exercises you can practise by yourself.

Try this one, breathing out as you go down. Legs straight!

Here Roger goes into a hurdle position – right knee well back. From this position he can stretch in several different directions. He can go forward, chin on knee; to the front, in between knees; or by twisting to his right he can bring his chin onto his pulled-back bent knee. Hold each position for ten seconds.

In this frog-like position, knees splayed, Jo . . .

. . . pushes back on her haunches. This is harder than it looks.

Just another way of stretching. From here . . .   . . . to here.

Or from here . . .   . . . to – Oh dear!

ISOMETRICS

A way of strengthening the muscles while stretching them is by isometric exercises. Each exercise should be repeated three times.

I push down on Roger's knees.

He now pushes up against my hands. I let him come up a few inches but no further. He continues to push for ten or fifteen seconds. When I push down again he finds he can stretch further than before.

Here, the object again is to increase flexibility and strength, in Jo's hips and legs.

Roger grips Jo's belt to give her stability and pushes her feet apart. From this full-stretched position Jo . . .

. . . pushes back. It's important that Roger allows each of Jo's feet to move in about six inches. Then he stops her movement and the real work begins. She pushes hard for ten or fifteen seconds and feels the tension increasing.

The next move shows the value of this isometric exercise. Roger begins again, pushing Jo's feet apart. She now finds she has a wider stretch than before.

Martin and I discuss a third example in the use of isometrics.

I push Jo's leg to its comfortable limit.

Jo pushes back but meets resistance. She will find, as before, that her flexibility has increased.

It's all here. Students begin this session by choosing their own exercises.

STRIKING OUT

Whether you are practising Taekwondo as a sport or in self-defence, you are unarmed. However, your body is equipped with 'weapons' you can use to block an attack and strike back. You will be taught how to use your body weapons correctly, how to punch, kick and strike in the most effective way.

In the sporting arena you pit your skills against an opponent. Contests are governed by rules and play must be kept safe. You will be shown the target areas of your opponent's body to strike at for point scoring.

There is a difference between scoring in a contest and retaliating against an assailant!

In defending yourself against an attacker (such as a mugger or a rapist) you do whatever is necessary to stop the attack. This may mean striking with your knee or fingers, which you would not do in Taekwondo as a sport.

TARGETS

I point out target areas on the human body for sport and self-defence.

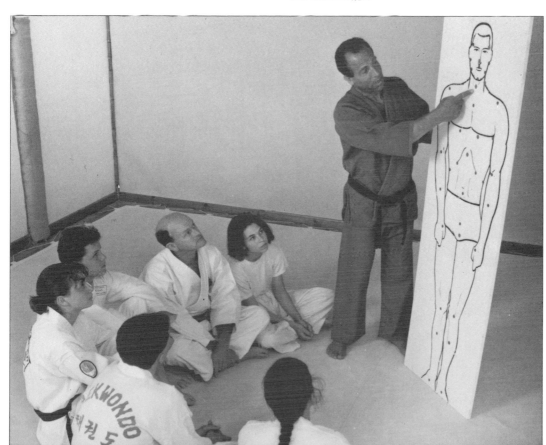

WEAPONS

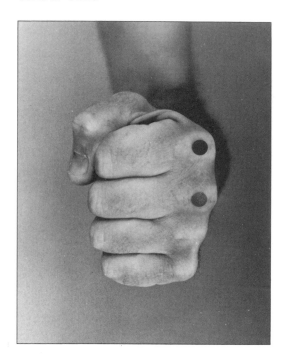

Forefist

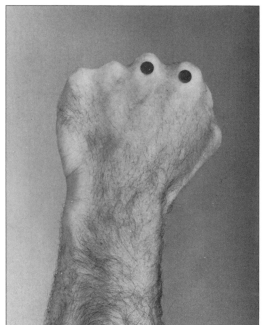

Backfist

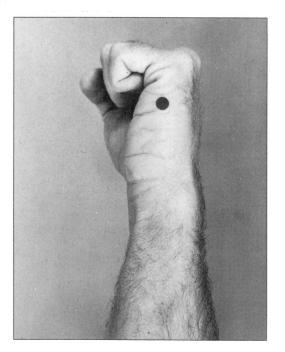

Sidefist

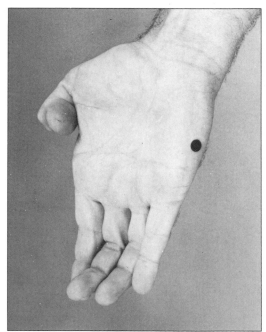

Knifehand

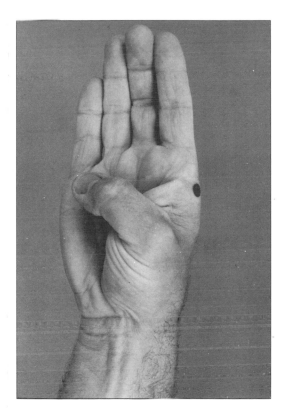

Reverse knifehand

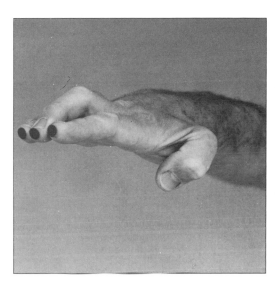

Fingertips

Heel of palm

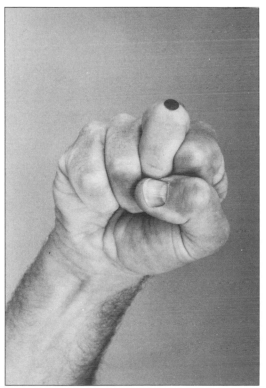

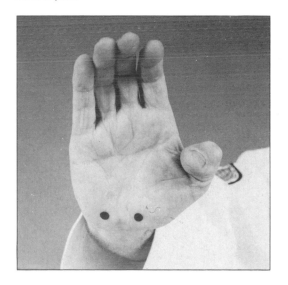

Knuckle

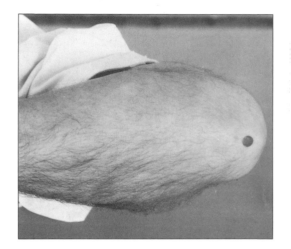

Elbow

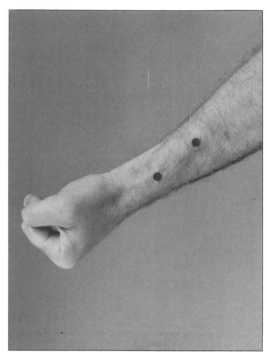

Inner forearm

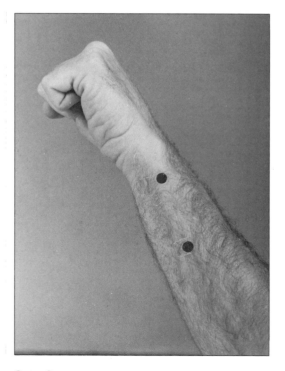

Outer forearm

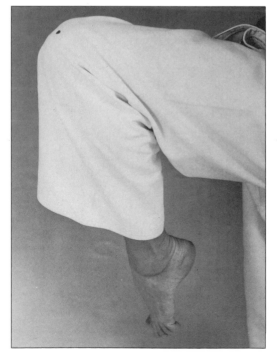

Knee

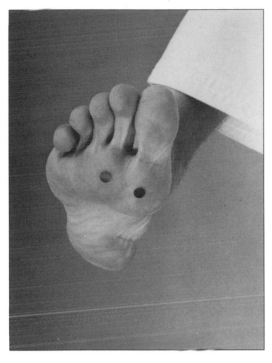

Ball of foot

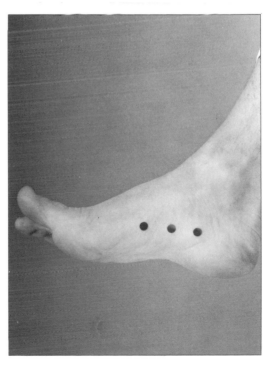

Base of heel

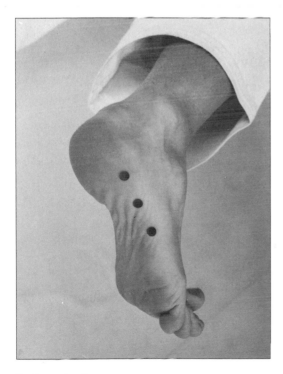

Footsword outer

Reverse footsword

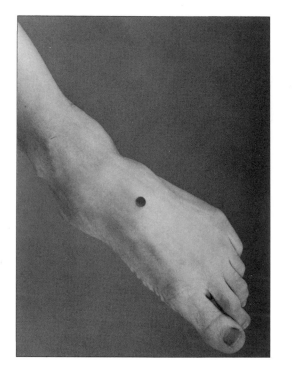

Instep

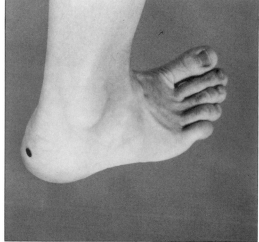

Back of heel

AT THE READY

To deliver an effective strike or defend with a block you need to be able to judge distance and act swiftly. To do this you must be in good balance and posture – that is, a good stance.

A good stance, although held only for a fraction of a second, will allow you either to execute your kick or punch or just move smoothly into another stance to avoid an attack. A boxer who gets his footwork wrong is often caught off guard and toppled over. The same applies in Taekwondo.

There are many different stances. Some are highly specialised, linked with certain techniques. Don't try anything fancy yet – you may find yourself flat on your back.

First you must learn a number of general stances. Some are upright, others low with knees bent. A lower stance can be more stable than a taller stance, while the more upright position can allow you to be more mobile. You need to be ready instantly to switch from one to another, and you will soon learn how to distribute your weight to achieve a stance from which you can either attack or defend.

Your instructor will have shown you the many different stances and their purposes – you adapt them to suit your body. Always remember that Taekwondo allows its practitioners freedom of movement and expression. Once you have understood the basic principles you can go on to master the art.

We now see six basic stances:

Ready stance – legs parallel.

Sitting or straddle stance.

Fighting stance, with 70 per cent of Martin's weight on his back leg.

Walking into a forward stance, with weight evenly distributed between his two legs.

Another ready stance. His leg is ready for action.

In this rear foot stance, Martin has blocked a blow with his left palm heel and is prepared to strike with his left leg.

Remember you need to be able to switch from one stance to another. Here Martin demonstrates how he transfers from a back stance to a forward stance.

With 70 per cent of his weight on his rear leg . . .

. . . he moves into . . .

. . . a forward stance with weight evenly distributed between both legs.

COMING TO BLOWS

13

THE MAKING OF A FIST

You've been through the stances and the weapons of the body. One of the most often used weapons is the hand formed into a fist. To make the fist into a highly scientific instrument it is essential to follow strict rules in its 'manufacture'

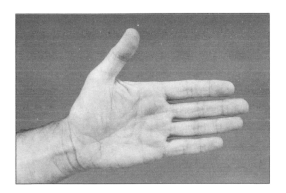

An open relaxed hand.

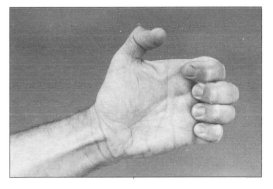

Roll the fingers tightly . . .

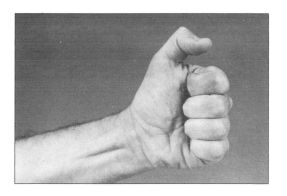

. . . pressing into the palm, starting with the little finger.

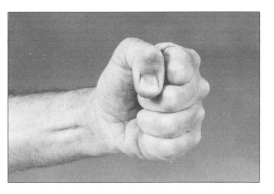

Place the thumb firmly on the index and middle finger.

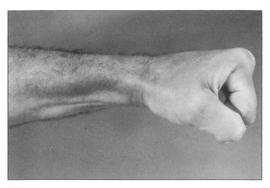

Left: **This is how your fist should look from the side. Notice that the top of the clenched fist is in line with the arm and forms a right angle with the index finger.**

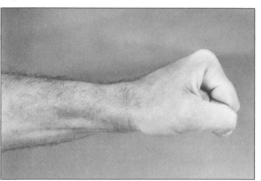

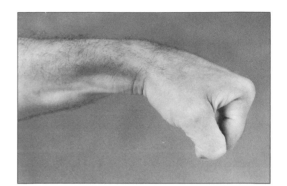

WRONG! A clenched fist bent at the wrist either upwards or downwards (*above right*) is weak and if used in an attack could cause you serious injury.

PUNCHING

Now for the punch.

Begin in a forward stance, left foot forward, knee slightly bent. Extend your left arm, fist clenched. Your right arm, hand formed into a fist, is at your right side, level with your belt. Hold your body upright: head, shoulders and hips should be forward-facing.

Step directly forward with the rear leg, letting it glide over the floor as it passes your left leg.

As you put down your foot (*above right*) bringing you into a right forward stance, several things happen at once. You withdraw your extended left arm, bringing your fist to your side; at the same time

you drive out your right hand. The two fists reach their new positions together. This is important.

With your rear leg straightened, locked in position, and the front leg firmly on the floor, you are in a good forward stance again. Check to see that your fists are correctly clenched. In practice, see that you are accurately aimed at your imaginary target.

Keep practising this stepping forward and punching technique. Hip movement plays a key role in many of the hand and foot techniques in Taekwondo. Some require the hips to twist; others, like this punch, need the hips to thrust through squarely.

You can also practise this punch from a straddle stance. At the moment of impact your body tenses, this concentrates force on your target.

HAND WEAPONS ON TARGET

There are many ways of using the fist.

Martin is ready for action.

This is a reverse punch, so called because the right arm is used with the left leg forward.

Martin aims a backfist to Roger's temple.

A turning punch to Roger's jaw.

This time the target is Roger's solar plexus with an upset punch.

The unclenched hand can be as damaging as the fist.

This is a palm heel strike to the jaw.

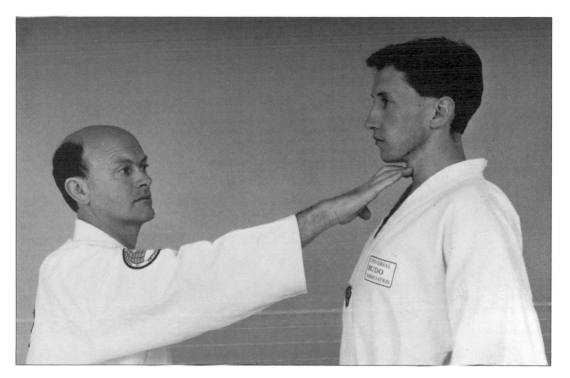

A fingertip thrust to the throat.

Martin attacks Roger's neck with a knifehand strike.

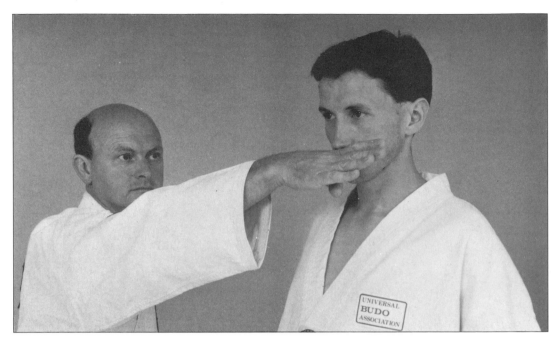

In this reverse knifehand attack, the hand comes up under the nose.

This elbow strike could also be targeted on the face or head.

KICKING

Taekwondo kicking techniques are physically more powerful than any in all the martial arts. In addition, they are spectacular. It is not unusual to see two exponents leaping through the air targeting kicks at one another.

The stretching exercises you do are vital to the development of kicking – they go together. Without pushing the leg and hip muscles beyond their normal use you will not be able to practise the dynamic kicking techniques of Taekwondo. These techniques come into play when your opponent is out of arm's reach and you cannot punch or strike.

Once your muscles, the sinews and tendons, have gained more elasticity, you can concentrate on the kick. The essence is to deliver the kick with power. Full power in all kicks will be realised only if you follow certain procedures. The hips are used to twist, thrust and drive power into each kick; the leg must be fully extended to deliver that power.

Let's start with a basic front kick.

Roger takes up a fighting stance. He brings his rear leg . . .

. . . forward, bent at the knee, with the sole of his foot parallel to the ground. In making this move his supporting foot has turned outwards. This allows Roger the maximum freedom for hip movement as he . . .

. . . drives out his leg, toes pulled back.

I repeat – the full power of your kick comes from the way you manage your hips. Your leg must only reach its full extension at the **point of impact**.

At present (as in punching) you are practising the kick in stages. You want to make the action smooth and continuous. You accelerate quickly, without hesitation, achieving maximum impact on contact with your target. As soon as you have landed on your target, withdraw your leg, bent at the knee. Then step back into a fighting stance, as you started.

Now you know what makes an effective kick you can practise other basic moves. These are more front kicks and also side and back kicks. The following pictures show different kicks, using different parts of the feet as weapons.

FRONT KICK

Jo faces up to Roger.

Toes pulled back, legs fully extended, she makes impact with a front kick.

Here, in making this front stamping kick, Jo is just about to thrust her hips forward and straighten her leg. This sends Roger reeling backwards.

Another front kick, using the instep of the foot.

SIDE KICK

From her fighting stance Jo is ready to pivot on her right leg.

She has turned sideways-on to Roger, hitting him in
the ribs with a footsword. This is known as a side-
piercing kick.

This time with the ball of her foot, Jo attacks Roger's
throat using a thrusting side kick.

There are other ways of coming into position for a
side kick.

Jo takes up a straddle stance.

With a little skip and raising her leg . . .

. . . she lands on target with another side-piercing
kick.

BACK KICK

From this one-legged stance Jo is ready to . . .

. . . kick back – into the solar plexus with the base of
her heel.

TURNING KICK

With the basic side, front and back kicks under your
belt (you will do these at early examinations) you can
progress onto more difficult moves. We begin with a
turning kick. The power of this kick comes from the
turning and twisting of the hips.

From a left fighting stance Jo will raise her right
foot, with knee bent, and bring it forward. At the
same time she will swivel on her front supporting
leg . . .

. . . leaning back and straightening her leg in this
spectacular swing. This curving movement brings the
ball of her foot on target.

REVERSE TURNING KICK

Roger is about to punch but he's in for a surprise.

As he lunges Jo pivots on her right forward leg. Her leg swings . . .

. . . round and . . .

back. And that's it – a reverse turning kick with her
back heel goes straight for the temple.

HOOKING KICK

From this straddle stance Jo is ready to execute a hooking kick.

Jo gives a little skip. This brings her rear leg to the position vacated by her front leg which now swings up and round in an arc.

This is a hook kick: the leg is at first bent at the knee in front of the body. The hooking action takes the heel of her foot to the target, Roger's neck.

TWISTING KICK

This is not easy – just look how the leg and foot twist!

AXE KICK

Another difficult technique, but not impossible. Keep stretching!

Kicking techniques of Taekwondo separate this martial art from the others, and none more so than the spectacular flying kick.

Flying side kick

Flying front kick. Eight foot up and still rising.

ON GUARD

14

A boxer spends much of his training time weaving and ducking, avoiding blows.

It also makes sense that in Taekwondo you first try to move out of the way of an oncoming punch or kick – evasion. If you are unable to get out of the way (either because you are not quick enough or do not have the room) then you need to be able to block an attack. This does not mean a direct clash. To meet force with force is not the answer; you could end up in more trouble. The power behind a kick could break a defender's arm.

A block is used to deflect an oncoming blow. Redirecting – that is, taking the power and sting out of a punch or kick – requires special attention. For maximum effect a block needs to be applied before the blow comes to full power or after it has missed its target and is slowing down. The defender avoids the blow and at the same time blocks it.

This puts the attacker in a weak, unbalanced position. Always be ready to follow up with a counter-move. This could be a punch, a kick, a throw, armlock or strangle. First we look at some basic blocks. We deal with other blocking and counter-moves in the later chapter on self-defence.

RISING BLOCK

Roger keeps his eyes on his opponent. He shifts his body back to avoid the oncoming blow and at the same time his hands swing . . .

. . . into play. One arm pushes the attacker's arm up and away from its target (Roger's face); the other hand comes to Roger's side ready for a counter-punch.

Here he has executed a low block in response to a punch or kick.

CROSS BLOCK

Roger prepares to block a downward blow to his head. Both arms are ready to thrust upward, twisting in front of his body . . .

. . . into a cross block. This block can also be used to stop a blow coming towards the face.

Here Roger has cross-blocked downwards to stop a kick.

INNER FOREARM BLOCK

Roger moves out of range of a punch ready to turn and . . .

. . . defend with an inner forearm block. Note that his left hand, clenched into a fist, is at his side, ready for action.

OUTER FOREARM BLOCK

This time Roger swings into action with . . .

. . . an outer forearm block. Note how the whole arm twists as it comes through to meet its target.

KNIFEHAND BLOCK

Roger is ready to swing round, arm rotating . . .   . . . for a knifehand block.

PALM HEEL BLOCK

The base of the palm is used to . . .

. . . knock the attacker's arm off course.

In all the above, evasion and body movement play a key role. There are other ways of blocking – with the elbow, the clenched fist forming a hammer, and so on. You may need to block against a punch or kick. The pictures that follow demonstrate some of the techniques in action.

Martin has struck downward at Roger's head. Roger has met the attack with a rising cross block. This has pushed the blow well off target.

Roger could have used a rising forearm block.

Here Roger deflects a punch with a knifehand block.

ON GUARD

Jo attempts to kick out at Martin with the instep of
her foot. Using a downward cross block Martin is in
the clear.

Here Martin parries a front kick with a downward
outer forearm block.

Jo's high side kick is 'slapped' away with a palm
block.

15

SET YOUR SIGHTS

Whether you practise Taekwondo for sport or for self-defence, you need to make sure that your punch, kick or strike is bang on line. You also need to know that in the face of real danger your attack will do the job by hitting hard enough.

One method of training to judge distance, timing and the power of impact is to use kick bags or focus pads. Some kick bags, particularly if they are large and heavy, can be suspended from the ceiling or from wall-mounted brackets. Other more manageable-sized bags can be held by a partner.

Whichever kind you use, kicking practice on these bags will bring some sense of reality into your efforts.

You'll be able to strike out with heel, footsword, instep and all the other weapons of your feet as well as using your hands. Punching and kicking in this way will not do you any damage; in fact your hands and feet will toughen up – good preparation for destruction techniques.

Focus pads are designed to be hand-held by a partner. If they are held at different heights you can strike with hands or feet, or combinations of both.

William squares up to Martin who is holding two focus pads as targets.

A backfist with William's left hand followed by . . .

. . . a straight punch with his right.

To test William's timing and focus, Martin will move the pads up and down, teaching William to think – and react quickly. To practise kicking techniques heavier duty pads are used.

William is well on target but he has left himself open to a successful counter-attack by not maintaining his balance and guard.

William switches . . .

. . . kicking out with his other leg. His balance is
better but what about that guard?

There are many other uses of pads.

Even with the protection of a heavy-duty pad, Martin feels the force of a powerful front kick.

A class trains with a variety of pads.

SPARRING

16

You have learnt the basic punches, strikes, blocks, kicks and stances. You know where and how to strike, and have practised with the kick bag and focus pads. Now for action with a partner.

But take care – basic sparring exercises are taken step by step. All the moves are pre-arranged. First you decide, with your partner, who will defend and who will attack and at which point you will swop roles. It is customary, to begin with anyway, to exchange roles after each series of moves.

In this chapter on sparring, we deal with different forms of pre-arranged moves. Later we move on to free sparring where, kitted out in safety gear, you attack and defend at will.

Pre-arranged (fixed) sparring is not 'soft'; it's just as demanding as free sparring. Practised correctly it can be extremely strenuous. When you are clear what each of you has to do, every move, attacking and defensive, should be applied with vigour.

Fixed sparring allows both the attacker and defender to experiment and sharpen their wits at the same time. The attacker soon learns how to put together a string of simultaneous attacks (combinations) using hands and feet, to the left and to the right, high and low. The defender's timing, distance and technical ability are put to the test – can he move out of the way, block, deflect and counter-attack?

Training in Taekwondo now steps up a gear. You'll see that your early and continued training in stamina, fitness and flexibility pays dividends. We begin with three-step sparring.

THREE-STEP SPARRING

Three-step sparring is a basic exercise to train students in the correct attacking and defensive techniques. This form of fixed sparring consists of three attacks met by three blocks and one counter-attack.

Study the following four series of pictures. They show three-step sparring in action. In each sequence, the attacker (Roger) steps forward punching right,

left, right. In all four he attacks with mid-section punches. This is a good line of attack to start with. Later on, strike out with high or low punches – and don't forget to attack kicking out with legs.

Martin (the defender) selects his block and sticks to it. Whichever he chooses – it could be a knifehand or forearm block – it can be made inside or outside of the attacking arm. Remember, when practising three-step sparring the aggressor always begins his attack striking out with either the right arm or right leg. However, the defender has a choice. He can step back with either leg and block with either arm.

This picture shows Roger in the ready position to make his punch.

Roger's first move, a right punch, meets an outer forearm block.

A left punch gets the same treatment.

Martin steps backwards again but enough's enough
and . . .

. . . he counter-attacks with a reverse punch.

Martin defends with a knifehand block.

Another knifehand block.

This time Martin retaliates with . . .

. . . a turning kick.

As in sequence one, Martin defends with an outer forearm block. However, this time he has stepped back with his left leg first and blocked inside the attacking arm.

Same again.

After Roger's third punch he expects a counter-attack from Martin who . . .

. . . pulls back his blocking arm. His left hand guards his face and his right (the former blocking arm) prepares to . . .

. . . spring a back fist to Roger's nose.

Martin steps back from Roger's punch, at the same time making a knifehand block.

Martin employs the same block each time Roger attacks.

Now having stepped back and blocked for the third time . . .

. . . Martin, keeping his target (Roger) in sight, goes
into . . .

. . . a reverse turning kick.

TWO-STEP SPARRING

You can go on practising three-step sparring, attacking, blocking and countering with techniques of your own choice. The next stage in fixed sparring is two-step. You are now preparing to defend yourself against attacks from hands and feet in a variety of combinations.

In the fixed exercise pictures here, the aggressor makes two attacks; the defender blocks and counter-attacks.

Jo and Martin square up. All Martin's attacks in the following sequences begin either with the right hand or right foot. He starts from this L stance.

Jo steps in to defend with an outer forearm rising block.

Martin kicks with his left leg. Jo steps back and cross-blocks, pressing down. This forces Martin to step forward leaving the way open for her to retaliate . . .

. . . with a twin vertical punch.

A right side punch from Martin is stopped with an upward palm heel block.

Now Martin tries a turning kick. Jo blocks this second attack with her outer forearm. She pushes away his leg and steps in . . .

. . . with a back elbow strike.

Martin comes out kicking. Jo cross-blocks, forcing his leg down.

Martin does not give up. He steps forward with a twin vertical punch. Jo stops this with an outer forearm wedging block.

Jo at once follows through with a knee strike. Ouch!

Martin attempts a finger-tip thrust at Jo's face. Jo diverts this with a knifehand rising block.

Martin makes a renewed attack, this time with a side kick. Jo, with a palm heel pushing block, spins him round into . . .

. . . a vulnerable position. She can either follow through with a kick or with the twin upset punch as shown here – or both!

Another palm heel block from Jo stops Martin's back kick.

Martin's second attack is with his open hand. Jo is ready for this with an outer forearm block followed by . . .

. . . a reverse knifehand strike.

Martin's high turning kick meets a twin straight forearm block.

He comes back with a hand strike. Jo checks it with a palm hooking block. She grabs his arm, pulls him towards her and . . .

. . . strikes with a side-piercing kick.

Jo's twin forearm guarding block saves her from Martin's side punch.

He attacks with a reverse turning kick. Jo moves well back.

One good turn deserves another. Jo's reverse turning kick is bang on target.

Martin still fails to make his mark with a well-aimed side kick. Jo goes for an inner forearm block. She pushes away Martin's leg.

He takes advantage of the momentum to swing completely round and strike out with a knifehand, but misses. Jo leaps in and counters . . .

. . . with a backfist.

SPARRING

ONE-STEP SPARRING

Three and two-step sparring have demonstrated the many ways there are of dealing with an attack. One-step sparring shows you how to block an attack and respond immediately; you don't give the attacker a chance to have a second go. One-step sparring can be divided into two forms of training. First, block and counter. Second, block and counter at the same time.

In the first method of one-step sparring shown here, Roger will attack. Jo will first defend with a block and then counter-attack.

Jo's outer forearm block is the first response to a
punch from Roger.

Her second response: she steps forward and twists,
delivering a powerful reverse punch.

Jo steps back, making a knifehand block.

Slipping her left foot forward, Jo lashes out with a reverse knifehand.

Stepping back (right leg), Jo blocks Roger's punch
with her outer forearm. She now steps forward with
her right leg and . . .

. . . hits Roger with an upset punch to the solar
plexus.

Jo moves back, making a palm-hooking block. She grabs Roger's wrist, pulling him forward to increase the impact of . . .

. . . her side-piercing kick.

Jo has distanced herself from Roger's attack but cleverly makes sure that she's not out of range for . . .

. . . her go at him!

Another outer forearm block from Jo checks Roger's
punch and opens the way for . . .

. . . her front stamping kick.

Fast footwork is the essence of Taekwondo. You have seen attacks and counter-attacks demonstrated, with our models making good use of their legs. In the sparring so far you have seen a single counter-attack. We now move forward to counter-attacks using combination kicking techniques.

Jo blocks with her foot.

This pushes Roger's hand away, opening him up for a side kick. She's not finished yet!

Her right leg comes back ready to fire again.

Another side kick, this time to the head.

Jo has knocked away Roger's hand.

She spins all the way round to her right and comes back with a reverse turning kick.

Roger's still not off the hook. Jo re-charges . . .

. . . and her second turning kick again goes straight to the head.

Now to the second form of training in one-step sparring – blocking and countering at the same time with instantaneous reaction.

Martin and Roger: peace before the storm.

Straight away Roger moves in with a knifehand block to Martin's punch and with a knifehand strike to Martin's neck. The two moves are made together.

A knifehand block and a palm heel strike to the chin.

Martin's arm is caught between two outer forearm blocks.

A knifehand block again from Roger. He also delivers a reverse knifehand to the groin.

Roger blocks; at the same time, his left leg reaches for the sky to bring his downward axe kick to Martin's head.

This really is clever stuff, the last thing Martin expected – a twisting kick!

There is no limit to the way in which you can deal with an attack. The following pictures show Roger demonstrating how he pursues his counter-attack to the point of flooring his opponent.

Outer forearm block.

Upset punch to the ribs.

Backfist to the temple.

Stamping kick to the back of the knee.

He's all yours.

FREE SPARRING

Three, two and one-step sparring will have taught you a lot about your reflexes, timing, control, technique, flexibility, stamina and fitness. You'll feel more relaxed when facing an opponent – more confident to deal with an attack.

Don't get too cool; you're going to begin free sparring. No fixed moves from now on! Free sparring is the first step towards real competition. Caution is necessary; as you will be striking out with hard techniques, rules are introduced. A head guard and groin protector and other sensible safety gear should be worn. You never know what's coming next; you may not be quick enough to stop that kick!

A fingertip thrust at the eyes or a kick to knee or groin may be the only answer to an unprovoked attack in the street. You will have practised these and other defence moves in one-step sparring. In free sparring and competition such techniques are not allowed.

Free sparring is the most demanding training. Only through trial and error (and a lot of sweat) will you be

able to overcome and deal with the variety of attacks you could expect. You may need to go back to the kick bag or focus pads to improve certain techniques. You now need to develop your own style of fighting; to find out what suits you requires constant practice.

Jo (left) has an idea.

Clauda has one too.

Free sparring practice gives us an opportunity to learn about rules. Your association will have its rule book – get a copy and study it.

Clauda (right) has broken a rule. I stop the fight and . . .

. . . signal the infringement with my right hand: 'You held Jo's leg'.

COMPETITION

17

Free sparring may have given you a taste for competition. Often, two local clubs will get together and run a friendly event, so why not join in?

Most organisations hold national and some international events, and area and regional trials may be held for selection to these events. Then there's the World Championships and the Olympic Games. You have to be a Black Belt to enter these, and to have proved yourself a worthy contender by success at national events.

Competitors fight in weight groups, men and women competing separately. The two forms of com-

petition, full contact and semi-contact, are equally demanding. Each contest is usually of three 3-minute rounds with a 1-minute break between rounds. A referee controls the contest and is supported by four corner judges who keep the scores.

In all competitions head protectors must be worn. In full contact bouts the hands and feet are not

The 1976 European Championships at Crystal Palace. Henk Meijer (right) was the only person to hold both the ITF and WTF world heavyweight titles.

Cathy Miles (left) and Au Tham Ying battle it out at the European Championships.

Flying high in the 1985 World Games.

covered. To protect opponents from the impact of blows, each competitor wears padded body armour, forearm and shin guards and a groin protector. But don't be fooled; even padded up you can still get knocked. Kicks and strikes, even if not delivered with full force (speed is more important) must land on target with noticeable impact.

A kick or punch that lands on target (the head or front or side of the upper body, but not the arms) scores a point. If a contestant stops or knocks down an opponent with a skilfully executed technique, he or she will also be awarded a point. Each time a point is awarded the contest is stopped and the score recorded by the judges. Penalty points may be incurred for executing, or even attempting, prohibited acts such as attacking with the knee or holding the opponent. In the event of a draw, the contestant who has scored the most points by kicking will be judged the winner. Taekwondo is renowned for its kicking techniques.

In semi-contact competitions the rules are different. There is still a referee with his four corner judges but the emphasis on how you score and the points awarded are of different value.

The idea here is again to punch and kick out at the body and head but not to make hard contact – you only demonstrate that you are on target. This requires a lot of skill and control both technically and physically. Those who take part in these semi-contact bouts like to demonstrate the effectiveness of their techniques by 'destruction' – breaking boards or even bricks with their bare hands and feet! Full contact players can also perform these feats.

It would be foolish to enter any form of Taekwondo competition without safety in mind. In semi-contact bouts head, hand and foot protectors are mandatory. Although protective body armour is not thought necessary as a mandatory piece of safety equipment (because you are not intending to hit hard), special chest protectors have been designed for women competitors. These are used in many combat sports. Groin, shin and forearm protectors may also be worn. A gum shield is a good idea.

As in full contact bouts, it is agreed that kicking techniques are the most difficult to execute and land on target. In semi-contact bouts this is recognised by awarding more points for a kick than a punch. A punch to the head, side or frontal upper area of the body (above the belt) will earn one point. A kick to the body earns two points and to the head, considered the most difficult, three points.

Points are awarded during the contest without interruption, so there is continuous fighting. Each corner judge keeps the score using two hand-held point clickers (one for each competitor) to tot up the scores. At the end of the two or three rounds, each judge signals to the referee which contestant they deem the winner and the referee makes the announcement by holding up the winner's hand.

Action pictures from the Seoul Olympics, 1988.

18

DESTRUCTION

In any martial art where the hands and feet are used as weapons, it is essential that a blow, strike or kick is delivered effectively – with accuracy and force. Taekwondo is a Korean military form of unarmed combat, and is used when no other weapon is available. Hand and foot techniques need to be put to the test. This is done by destruction – breaking techniques.

Many people see these destruction techniques such as breaking stacks of tiles, bricks, wooden boards or even blocks of ice, as spectacular feats. To see a martial artist smash through six concrete blocks with his bare hands is indeed spectacular, and in Karate, Kung Fu and other arts, such feats are not part of any normal training programme and are often done for showmanship.

In Taekwondo, however, breaking techniques are part of training. Testing the efficiency of strikes, kicks and punches by directing them at wooden boards is a requirement for passing a grade (usually blue belt) and promotion to the next level. Don't worry; by the time you are a blue belt you will be able confidently to strike at a one-inch thick piece of board. This may seem a daunting prospect now, but you'll be surprised; when it comes to it, it won't seem so frightening and you'll do it. The kick bags have given you (and your partner) a good indication of the force behind your kicking and punching techniques. It is

Louise is no heavyweight but she confidently measures up to the wooden board.

She goes in with all of her six stone behind her
and . . .

. . . the board is in pieces!

now a matter of focusing, concentrating all that force of your kick or punch on a specific point on the board – your target. It's not just a matter of physical strength. Any strong person can smash his fist into a pile of boards, but without training it is unlikely that he would be able to break them; he's more likely to injure himself.

Through your training – press-ups on knuckles, punching at pads – you will have safely, maybe unknowingly, toughened up your hands. Training bare-footed on the floor and kicking out at bags will have toughened your feet. All you need do now is condition your mind. Concentration is a key point.

Focus on the target at the point you are going to strike and devote your whole mind to what you are doing. Now with accuracy, speed and power – strike! Tense your body as you hit the target. It is quite an achievement breaking that first board. Later on you will be able to break boards using hands or feet and maybe smash through thicker boards. But to begin with, use only the thinnest of boards.

Jo's side-piercing kick smashes through the board as smartly as her sister Louise's elbow strike.

Martin holds the board – a challenge to Roger.

Roger makes a turning kick. The ball of his foot does the job.

19

SELF-DEFENCE

There are many rules governing Taekwondo competition. The contest area has to be a certain size, the contestants' uniform must fit correctly. In Taekwondo sport you are out to win. You can attack and make mistakes, but you'll only lose points.

In self-defence there are no points, no rules. Self-defence is for real.

Taekwondo grew from a need for self-defence. You, as a practitioner of Taekwondo, know that outside the sporting arena you must not provoke or instigate an attack. However, if you need to defend yourself, you do what is necessary to stop the attack. This may mean using a simple but effective block.

A well-executed block could, as you know, inflict sufficient pain on an attacker to deter him from pur-

suing his attack. If you have not stopped him, you could resort to one of the many counter-attacks you have learned. Some of these counter-attacks are easily recognised as those used only in self-defence.

Techniques in this section are for self-defence only, not for sport. Some of the initial moves will be familiar to you; they have been shown earlier in the book. However, following the Taekwondo moves, I show locks, strangles and throws that you may not know so well. These will fit nicely into your Taekwondo programme.

I await Martin's attack.

Martin steps forward, punching. I move in, avoiding the blow and at the same time striking with a reverse knife hand.

I keep moving in; my right leg takes up a position behind Martin's right leg. My hands clasp tightly under his right arm and around his neck. I pull in my arms, effecting a strangle, and . . .

. . . stepping forward with my left leg I topple Martin backwards . . .

. . . to the floor.

I meet Martin's punch with a rising outer forearm block. I pivot to my left and grip his hand at the wrist.

My left hand clasps his elbow. With a rolling arm movement, while . . .

. . . stepping forward, I lock his elbow at the joint . . .

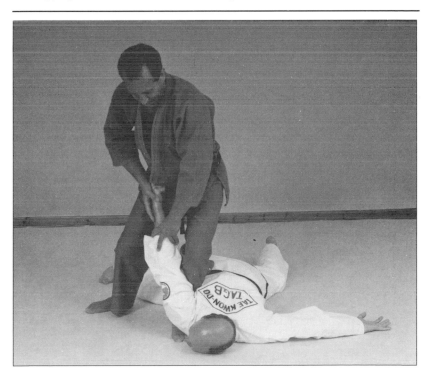

. . . forcing him to the ground. From start to finish
this is one continuous movement.

I avoid Martin's fingertip thrust. Note my forward
stance.

I turn to grasp Martin's wrist. I keep his palm
uppermost and lift his arm as I step . . .

. . . forward. From this stance I start to move
upright and . . .

. . . at the same time I lever his arm over my
shoulder. The pain to Martin's shoulder and arm is
considerable; the muscles and joints are under great
strain. Take care!

I step in and block Martin's attack with my outer forearm.

I now do two things. My clenched fist opens to a knifehand, striking into Martin's neck. My left hand traps his arm against my shoulder.

I step back onto my right leg. My right hand covers
his elbow. With his arm now trapped against my
shoulder, I press downward on his arm. This locks
the elbow joint.

I continue my downward pressure. Result –
immobilisation!

I avoid Martin's side kick. My left hand has blocked
his leg – I use an outer forearm block.
   Then come these simultaneous motions:

I scoop up his leg, make a palm heel strike to his jaw
and step behind his supporting leg.

I push at Martin's chin. The leg I scooped I now lift
up. The leg I have placed behind Martin's I sweep
back. He can only go one way – . . .

. . . to the ground.

I have side-stepped Martin's attack and grabbed his wrist. My left arm is ready, bent at the elbow.

I pull him forwards, stepping to his side and strike his throat with my elbow.

I now straighten my arm. Martin is unbalanced. I
push him backwards . . .

. . . and he goes to the ground.

JO'S STORY

20

You don't have to be special to get into Taekwondo. It took pressure from Joanne Hopper's father, Martin, before she and her sister Louise would even visit the local club to see what it was all about.

'I haven't looked back since,' says Jo, 'I was hooked.'

Jo was twelve then. Soon after this she was entering competitions and winning prizes. In the eight years since those early days, she has amassed the collection you see in the picture. Her most treasured trophy is for the English championship, won in 1987, which she has since successfully defended and still holds.

'My ambition is to fight for Great Britain in internationals,' she says. 'I know the training for this is hard and calls for perseverance, but I'm prepared for that.'

But Jo says that even women who do not have the same ambition need more encouragement in the martial arts. 'There are other things apart from competition. I also enjoy the sense of fitness and the self-defence aspect.'

PATTERNS

21

This section is mainly for reference. It covers nine International Taekwondo Federation patterns (*Tuls*) and eight World Taekwondo Federation patterns (*Taegeuks*).

All patterns should begin and end at precisely the same spot on the floor. This will indicate the performer's accuracy. Here is a method of achieving this accuracy:

Whichever way you face at the start of your pattern, call it north. Identify north by some object in front of you. It could be your examiner, a chair, a door, a window etc. With north in front of you, you know that south is behind you, west is to your left and east to your right. If, in the course of performing your pattern, you should get lost, you can re-orientate yourself by referring to north.

An example:
1. You are standing at START in a ready stance facing north.
2. Your first instruction is to turn west (90° turn to your left).
3. Your second instruction is to step west (a step forward).
4. Your third instruction is to turn east (180° about turn).
5. If your fourth instruction is to turn north, you know you must turn to the direction you were facing at the start.

The more techniques you learn in class, the more varied and complex the patterns become. You will be asked to demonstrate these patterns at grading examination. The higher the belt colour you are seeking, the more complicated the pattern and the greater the need for precision.

Patterns can be highly stylised, being performed almost like a dance, each movement leading to the next without interruption. Because this is a solo exercise, a pattern allows you to use potentially dangerous techniques in complete safety. They can look spectacular, dynamic and graceful.

You may find yourself so fascinated by your training in patterns that you decide to specialise and enter the many pattern competitions organised by various organisations.

WORLD TAEKWONDO FEDERATION TAEGEUKS – ONE TO EIGHT

All the eight *taegeuks* that follow are performed within the shape illustrated in diagram A.

Diagram A

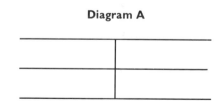

Now look at diagram B. I have added **North, South, East** and **West** as an easy guide to the instructions for each *taeguk*. The value of this diagram will become clear with your first move.

Diagram B

```
              N
W3 ─────────────┼───────────── E3

W2 ─────────────┼───────────── E2

WI ──────── START ──────── E2
              S
```

TAEGEUK 1

No.	Move	Stance	Action	Section
	To begin	ready		
1	turn W1	walk	outer left arm block	low
2	step W1	walk	right fist punch	mid
3	turn E1	walk	outer right arm block	low
4	step E1	walk	left fist punch	mid
5a	turn N	front	outer left arm block	low
5b			right fist punch	mid
6	turn E2	walk	inner left arm reverse block	mid
7	step E2	walk	right fist reverse punch	mid
8	turn W2	walk	inner right arm reverse block	mid
9	step W2	walk	left fist reverse punch	mid
10a	turn N	front	outer right arm block	low
10b			left fist punch	mid
11	turn W3	walk	outer left arm rising block	high
12a			right front kick	mid
12b	land W3	walk	right fist punch	mid
13	turn E3	walk	outer right arm rising block	high
14a			left front kick	mid
14b	land E3	walk	left fist punch	mid
15	turn S	front	outer left arm block	low
16	step S	front	right fist punch/kihap	mid
	To end	ready	pivot on right foot	

TAEGEUK 2

No.	Move	Stance	Action	Section
	To begin	ready		
1	turn W1	walk	outer left arm block	low
2	step W1	front	right arm punch	mid
3	turn E1	walk	outer right arm block	low
4	step E1	front	left fist punch	mid
5	turn N	walk	inner right arm reverse block	mid
6	step N	walk	inner left arm reverse block	mid
7	turn W2	walk	outer left arm block	low
8a			right front kick	mid
8b	land W2	front	right fist punch	high
9	turn E2	walk	outer right arm block	low
10a			left front kick	mid
10b	land E2	front	left fist punch	high
11	turn N	walk	outer left arm rising block	high
12	step N	walk	outer right arm rising block	high
13	turn E 3	walk	inside right arm reverse block	mid
14	turn W3	walk	inside left arm reverse block	mid
15	turn S	walk	outer left arm block	low
16a			right front kick	mid
16b	land S	walk	right fist punch	mid
17a			left front kick	mid
17b	land S	walk	left fist punch	mid
18a			right front kick	mid
18b	land S	walk	right fist punch/kihap	mid
	To end	ready	pivot on right foot	

TAEGEUK 3

No.	Move	Stance	Action	Section
	To begin	ready		
1	turn W1	walk	outer left arm block	low
2a			right front kick	mid
2b	land W1	front	double punch	mid
3	turn E1	walk	outer right arm block	low
4a			left front kick	mid
4b	land E1	front	double punch	mid
5	turn N	walk	inward right knifehand strike	high
6	step N	walk	inner left knifehand strike	high
7	turn W2	back	left knifehand block	mid
8		front	right reverse punch	mid
9	turn E2	back	right knifehand block	mid
10		front	left reverse punch	mid
11	turn N	walk	inner reverse right arm block	mid
12	step N	walk	inner reverse left arm block	mid
13	turn E3	walk	outer left arm block	low
14a			right front kick	mid
14b	land E3	front	double punch	mid
15	turn W3	walk	outer right arm block	low
16a			left front kick	mid
16b	land W3	front	double punch	mid
17a	turn S	walk	outer left arm block	low
17b			right reverse punch	mid
18a	step S	walk	outer right arm block	low
18b		walk	left reverse punch	mid
19a			left front kick	mid
19b	land S	walk	outer left arm block	low
19c		walk	right reverse punch	mid
20a			right front kick	mid
20b	land S	walk	outer right arm block	low
20c		walk	left reverse punch/kihap	mid
	To end	ready	pivot on right foot	

TAEGEUK 4

No.	Move	Stance	Action	Section
	To begin	ready		
1	turn WI	back	double knifehand block	mid
2	step WI	front	left palm block/right spearfinger	mid
3	turn EI	back	double knifehand block	mid
4	step EI	walk	right palm block/left spearfinger	mid
5	turn N	front	left knifehand rising block/right knifehand strike	high
6a			right front kick	mid
6b	land N	front	left reverse punch	mid
7			left side kick	mid
8a	step N		right side kick	mid
8b	land N	back	double knifehand block	mid
9	turn E3	back	outer left arm block	mid
10a			right front kick	mid
10b	land W3	back	inner right reverse block	mid
11	turn W3	back	outer right arm block	mid
12a			left front kick	mid
12b	land E3	back	inner reverse left arm block	mid
13	turn S	front	left knifehand rising block/right knifehand strike	high
14a			right front kick	mid
14b	land S	front	right backfist	high
15	turn E2	walk	inner left arm block	mid
16		walk	right reverse punch	mid
17	turn W2	walk	inner right arm block	mid
18		walk	left reverse punch	mid
19a	turn S	front	inner left arm block	mid
19b		front	double punch	mid
20a	step S	front	inner right arm block	mid
20b		front	double punch	mid
	To end	ready	pivot on right foot	

TAEGEUK 5

No.	Move	Stance	Action	Section
	To begin	ready		
1	turn W1	front	left arm block	low
2		ready	left downward hammer fist	high
3	turn E1	front	right arm block	low
4		ready	right downward hammer fist	high
5a	turn N	front	inner left arm block	mid
5b		front	inner right reverse arm block	mid
6a			right front kick	mid
6b	land N	front	right backfist strike	high
6c		front	inner left arm reverse block	mid
7a			left front kick	mid
7b	land N	front	left backfist strike	high
8	step N	front	right backfist	high
9	turn E3	back	left knifehand block	mid
10	step E3	walk	right elbow strike	high
11	turn W3	back	right knifehand block	mid
12	step W3	walk	left elbow strike	high
13a	turn S	front	outer left arm block	low
13b		front	inner right arm reverse block	mid
14a			right front kick	mid
14b	land S	front	outer right arm block	low
14c		front	inner left arm reverse block	mid
15	turn E2	front	outer left rising block	high
16a			right side kick	mid
16b	land E2	front	left elbow reverse strike	mid
17	turn W2	front	outer right arm rising block	high
18a			left side kick	mid
18b	land W2	front	right elbow reverse strike	mid
19a	turn S	front	outer left arm block	low
19b		front	inner right arm reverse block	mid
20a			right front kick	mid
20b	jump S	twist	right backfist strike/kihap	high
	To end	ready	pivot on right foot	

TAEGEUK 6

No.	Move	Stance	Action	Section
	To begin	ready		
I	turn WI	walk	outer right arm block	low
2a			right front kick	mid
2b	land EI	back	outer left arm block	mid
3	turn EI	walk	outer right arm block	low
4a			left front kick	mid
4b	land WI	back	outer right arm block	mid
5	turn N	front	right reverse knifehand block	high
6			right turning kick	mid
7a	land W2	walk	outer left arm block	high
7b		walk	right reverse punch	mid
8a			right front kick	mid
8b	land W2	front	left reverse punch	mid
9a	turn E2	front	outer right arm block	high
9b		front	left reverse punch	mid
10a			left front kick	mid
10b	land E2	front	right reverse punch	mid
II	turn N	ready	twin forearm side block	low
12	step N	front	left reverse knifehand block	high
13			left turning kick	mid
14	turn W3	front	outer right arm block	low
15a			left front kick	mid
15b	step E3	back	outer right arm block	mid
16	turn E3	front	outer left arm block	low
17a			right front kick	mid
17b	step W3	back	left outer forearm block	mid
18	turn N	back	double knifehand block	mid
19	step S	back	double knifehand block	mid
20a	step S	front	left palm block	mid
20b		front	right reverse punch	mid
21a	step S	front	right palm block	mid
21b	step S	front	left reverse punch	mid
	To end	ready	pull right foot back	

TAEGEUK 7

No.	Move	Stance	Action	Section
	To begin	ready		
1	turn W1	tiger	right reverse palm block	mid
2a			right front kick	mid
2b	step E1	tiger	inner left arm block	mid
3	turn E1	tiger	left reverse palm block	mid
4a			left front kick	mid
4b	step W1	tiger	inner right arm block	mid
5	turn N	back	double knitehand block	low
6	step N	back	double knifehand block	low
7	turn W2	tiger	right reverse palm block	mid
8		tiger	right back fist	high
9	turn E2	tiger	left palm block	mid
10		tiger	left back fist	high
11	turn N	close	left on right fist	high
12a	step N	front	twin forearm block	low/mid
12b		front	change hand positions	low/mid
13a	step N	front	twin forearm block	low/mid
13b		front	change hand positions	low/mid
14	turn E3	front	twin forearm block	high
15a			right knee strike	mid
15b	jump E3	twist	twin upset punch	mid
16	step W3	walk	cross block	low
17	turn W3	front	twin forearm block	high
18a			left knee strike	mid
18b	jump W3	twist	twin upset punch	mid
19	step E3	front	cross block	low
20	turn S	walk	left side backfist	high
21a			right inner crescent kick	high
21b	land S	horse	right elbow strike	mid
22	step S	walk	right side backfist	high
23a			left inner crescent kick	high
23b	step S	horse	left elbow strike	mid
24		horse	left knifehand block	mid
25	step S	horse	right punch/kihap	mid
	To end	ready	pivot on right foot	

TAEGEUK 8

No.	Move	Stance	Action	Section
	To begin	ready		
Ia	step N	back	outer forearm guarding block	mid
Ib		front	right reverse punch	mid
2a	jump N		left flying front kick/kihap	mid
2b	land N	front	left inner arm block	mid
2c		front	double punch	mid
3	step N	front	right punch	mid
4	turn W3	front	double arm block	high/low
5	turn E3	front	right upper cut	high
6	step E3	front	double arm block	high/low
7	turn W3	front	left upper cut	high
8	step S (face N)	back	left knifehand guarding block	mid
9		walk	right reverse punch	mid
10a			right front kick	mid
10b	slide N	tiger	right palm block	mid
11	turn W2	tiger	left knifehand guarding block	mid
12a			left front kick	mid
12b	land W2	front	right reverse punch	mid
13	slide E2	tiger	left palm block	mid
14	turn E2	tiger	right knifehand guarding block	mid
15a			right front kick	mid
15b	land E2	front	left reverse punch	mid
16	slide W2	tiger	right palm block	mid
17	turn S	tiger	double arm block	low
18a			left front kick	mid
18b	jump S		right front kick	high
18c	land S	front	inner right arm block	mid
18d		front	left reverse punch	mid
19	turn WI	back	left knifehand block	mid
20		front	right elbow strike	high
21a			right backfist	high
21b		front	left punch	mid
22	turn EI	back	right knifehand block	mid
23		walk	left elbow strike	high
24a		walk	left backfist	high
24b		walk	right punch	mid
	To end	ready	pull left foot	

INTERNATIONAL TAEKWONDO FEDERATION

TULS

Chon-ji
Dan-gun
Do-san
Won-hyo
Yul-gok
Joong-gun
Toi-gye
Hwa-rang
Choong-moo

All these patterns (*tuls*) again use **North, South, East** and **West** as before. However, when you perform these patterns you will find that the shapes vary. The shape of each *tul* is shown with the instructions.

CHON-JI TUL

No.	Move	Stance	Action	Section
	To begin	parallel ready		
1	turn west	walking	outer forearm block	low
2	step west	walking	obverse punch	mid
3	step east	walking	outer forearm block	low
4	step east	walking	obverse punch	mid
5	turn north	walking	outer forearm block	low
6	step north	walking	obverse punch	mid
7	step south	walking	outer forearm block	low
8	step south	walking	obverse punch	mid
9	turn east	L	inner forearm block	mid
10	step east	walking	obverse punch	mid
11	step west	L	inner forearm block	mid
12	step west	walking	obverse punch	mid
13	turn south	L	inner forearm block	mid
14	step south	walking	obverse punch	mid
15	step north	L	inner forearm block	mid
16	step north	walking	obverse punch	mid
17	step north	walking	obverse punch	mid
18	step south	walking	obverse punch	mid
19	step south	walking	obverse punch	mid
	To end	parallel ready	left foot moves	

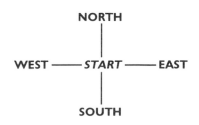

```
              NORTH
                |
WEST ——— START ——— EAST
                |
              SOUTH
```

PATTERNS

DAN-GUN TUL

No.	Move	Stance	Action	Section
	To begin	parallel ready		
1	turn west	L	knifehand guarding block	mid
2	step west	walking	obverse punch	high
3	step east	L	knifehand guarding block	mid
4	step east	walking	obverse punch	high
5	turn north	walking	outer forearm block	low
6	step north	walking	obverse punch	high
7	step north	walking	obverse punch	high
8	step north	walking	obverse punch	high
9	turn east	L	twin forearm block	high/mid
10	step east	walking	obverse punch	high
11	step west	L	twin forearm block	high/mid
12	step west	walking	obverse punch	high
13	turn south	walking	outer forearm block	low
14		walking	rising block	high
15	step south	walking	rising block	high
16	step south	walking	rising block	high
17	step south	walking	rising block	high
18	turn west	L	knifehand strike	mid
19	step west	walking	obverse punch	high
20	turn east	L	knifehand strike	mid
21	step east	walking	obverse punch	high
	To end	parallel ready	left foot moves	

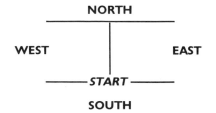

NORTH

WEST   EAST

—— START ——

SOUTH

DO-SAN TUL

No.	Move	Stance	Action	Section
	To begin	parallel ready		
1	turn west	walking	outer forearm block	high
2		walking	reverse punch	mid
3	turn east	walking	outer forearm block	high
4		walking	reverse punch	mid
5	turn north	L	knifehand guarding block	mid
6	step north	walking	right straight finger tip thrust	mid
7	step north	walking	back fist	high
8	step north	walking	back fist	high
9	turn east	walking	outer forearm block	high
10		walking	reverse punch	mid
11	turn west	walking	outer forearm block	high
12		walking	reverse punch	mid
13	turn S/S/E	walking	wedging block	high
14	step S/S/E		front snap kick	mid
15		walking	obverse punch fast	mid
16		walking	reverse punch fast	mid
17	turn S/S/W	walking	wedging block	high
18	step S/S/W		front snap kick	mid
19		walking	obverse punch fast	mid
20		walking	reverse punch fast	mid
21	turn south	walking	rising block	high
22	step south	walking	rising block	high
23	turn north	sitting	knifehand strike	mid
24	step east	sitting	knifehand strike	mid
	To end	parallel ready	right foot moves	

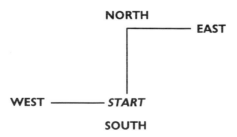

WON-HYO TUL

No.	Move	Stance	Action	Section
	To begin	close ready A		
1	turn west	L	twin forearm guarding block	high/mid
2		L	inward knifehand strike	high
3	slip left foot	fixed	side punch	mid
4	step east	L	twin forearm guarding block	high/mid
5		L	inward knifehand strike	high
6	slip right foot	fixed	side punch	mid
7	turn north	bending ready	outer forearm block	mid
8			side piercing kick	mid
9		L	knifehand guarding block	mid
10	step north	L	knifehand guarding block	mid
11	step north	L	knifehand guarding block	mid
12	step north	walking	straight finger tip thrust	mid
13	turn west	L	twin forearm	high/mid
14		L	inward knifehand strike	high
15	slip left foot	fixed	side punch	mid
16	step east	L	twin forearm	high/mid
17		L	inward knifehand strike	high
18	slip right foot	fixed	side punch	mid
19	step south	walking	circular block	low/mid
20	step south		front snap kick	low
21		walking	reverse punch	mid
22		walking	circular block	low/mid
23	step south		front snap kick	low
24		walking	reverse punch	mid
25		bending ready	outer forearm block	mid
26			side piercing kick	mid
27	turn west	L	outer forearm guarding block	mid
28	step east	L	outer forearm guarding block	mid
	To end	close ready A	right foot moves	

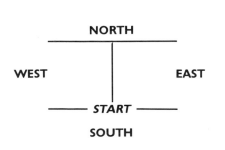

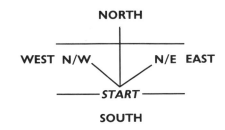

YUL-GOK TUL

No.	Move	Stance	Action	Section
	To begin	parallel ready		
1	left foot moves	sitting	left fist, set distance	mid
2		sitting	right punch fast	mid
3		sitting	left punch fast	mid
4	step east	sitting	right fist, set distance	mid
5		sitting	left punch fast	mid
6		sitting	right punch fast	mid
7	turn N.E	walking	inner forearm block	high
8	step N.E		front snap kick	low
9		walking	obverse punch fast	mid
10		walking	reverse punch fast	mid
11	turn N/W	walking	inner forearm block	high
12	step N/W		front snap kick	low
13		walking	obverse punch fast	mid
14		walking	reverse punch fast	mid
15	turn north	walking	obverse palm hooking block	high
16		walking	reverse palm hooking block	high
17		walking	obverse punch	mid
18	step north	walking	obverse palm hooking block	high
19		walking	reverse palm hooking block	high
20		walking	obverse punch	mid
21	step north	walking	obverse punch	mid
22		bending ready	outer forearm guarding block	mid
23			side piercing kick	mid
24		walking	front elbow strike	
25	turn south	bending ready	outer forearm guarding block	mid
26			side kick	mid
27		walking	front elbow strike	
28	turn east	L	twin knifehand block	high/mid
29	step east	walking	straight finger tip thrust	mid
30	turn west	L	twin knifehand block	high/mid
31	step west	walking	straight finger tip thrust	mid
32	turn south	walking	outer forearm block	high
33		walking	reverse punch	mid
34	step south	walking	outer forearm block	high
35		walking	reverse punch	mid
36	jump south	X	left back fist strike	high
37	turn east	walking	double forearm block	high
38	step west	walking	double forearm block	high
	To end	parallel ready	left foot moves	

See left for diagram

PATTERNS

JOONG-GUN TUL

No.	Move	Stance	Action	Section
	To begin	close ready B		
1	turn west	L	reverse knifehand block	mid
2			front kick	low
3	step west	rear foot	upward palm heel block	mid
4	turn east	L	reverse knifehand block	mid
5			front kick	low
6	step east	rear foot	upward palm heel block	mid
7	turn north	L	knife hand guarding block	mid
8		walking	upper elbow strike	high
9	step north	L	knife hand guarding block	mid
10		walking	upper elbow strike	high
11	step north	walking	twin vertical punch	high
12	step north	walking	twin upset punch	mid
13	turn south	walking	cross fist rising block	high
14	turn east	L	back fist fast	high
15			left fist release fast	
16		walking	reverse punch	high
17	step west	L	back fist fast	high
18			right fist release fast	
19		walking	reverse punch	high
20	step south	walking	double forearm block	high
21		L	side punch	mid
22	step south		side piercing kick	mid
23		walking	double forearm block	high
24		L	side punch	mid
25	step south		side piercing kick	mid
26		L	outer forearm guarding block	mid
27		low	pressing block slow	low/mid
28	step south	L	outer forearm guarding block	mid
29		low	pressing block slow	low/mid
30	turn east	close	right fist moves slow to	left chest
31		fixed	U-shaped block	
32	step west	fixed	U-shaped block	
	To end	close ready B	left foot moves	

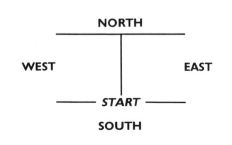

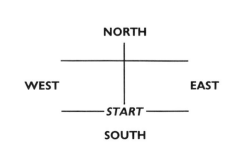

TOI-GYE TUL

No.	Move	Stance	Action	Section
	To begin	close ready B		
1	turn west	L	inner forearm block	mid
2		walking	upset finger tip thrust	low
3	turn north	close	left forearm block slow	low
			right rear backfist slow	high
4	turn east	L	inner forearm block	mid
5		walking	upset finger tip thrust	low
6	turn north	close	right forearm block slow	low
			left rear backfist slow	high
7	step north	walking	cross fist pressing block	low
8		walking	twin vertical punch	high
9			front snap kick	mid
10	step north	walking	obverse punch fast	mid
11		walking	reverse punch fast	mid
12	turn west	close	fists simultaneously slow to	hips
13	turn south	sitting	W-shaped outer forearm block	high
14	step west	sitting	W-shaped outer forearm block	high
15	step east	sitting	W-shaped outer forearm block	high
16	step east	sitting	W-shaped outer forearm block	high
17	step east	sitting	W-shaped outer forearm block	high
18	step west	sitting	W-shaped outer forearm block	high
19	step north	L	double inner forearm pushing block	low
20		walking	hands up to grab opponents	head
21			knee strike pull hands down	mid
22	turn south	L	knifehand guarding block	mid
23			front leg front snap kick	low
24		walking	flat finger tip thrust	high
25	step south	L	knifehand guarding block	mid
26			front leg front snap kick	low
27		walking	flat finger tip thrust	high
28	step north	L	rear back fist	high
29	jump south	X	cross fist pressing block	low
30	turn south	walking	double forearm block	high
31	turn west	L	knifehand guarding block	low
32		walking	circular block	low/mid
33	step east	L	knifehand guarding block	low
34		walking	circular block	low/mid
35	turn N/W	walking	circular block	low/mid
36	turn east	walking	circular block	low/mid
37	step north	sitting	right punch	mid
	To end	close ready B	right foot moves	

See left for diagram

PATTERNS

HWA-RANG TUL

No.	Move	Stance	Action	Section
	To begin	close ready C		
1	left foot moves	sitting	left palm pushing block	mid
2		sitting	right punch fast	mid
3		sitting	left punch fast	mid
4	turn east	L	twin forearm guarding block	high/mid
5		L	left upward punch	high
6	slide east	fixed	side punch	mid
7	pull right foot	vertical	knifehand downward strike	high
8	step east	walking	obverse punch	mid
9	turn north	walking	outer forearm block	low
10	step north	walking	obverse punch	mid
11	(Pull left foot to right while bringing left palm onto right forefist bending right elbow slightly)			
12			front leg side kick	mid
		L	knifehand strike	mid
13	step north	walking	obverse punch	mid
14	step north	walking	obverse punch	mid
15	turn east	L	knifehand guarding block	mid
16	step east	walking	straight finger tip thrust	mid
17	turn west	L	knifehand guarding block	mid
18			right turning kick fast	high
19			left turning kick fast	high
		L	knifehand guarding block	mid
20	turn south	walking	outer forearm block	low
21	pull left foot	L	reverse punch	mid
22	step south	L	reverse punch	mid
23	step south	L	reverse punch	mid
24	left foot slips	walking	cross fist pressing block	low
25	step south	L	right side elbow thrust to south	mid
26	turn west	close	right inner forearm block	mid
		close	left outer forearm block	low
27		close	(change position of hands)	
28		L	knifehand guarding block	mid
29	step east	L	knifehand guarding block	mid
	To end	close ready C	right foot moves	

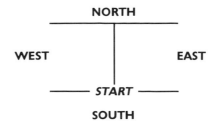

```
            NORTH
       ───────┬───────
              │
  WEST         │          EAST
              │
       ─── START ───
            SOUTH
```

CHOONG-MOO TUL

No.	Move	Stance	Action	Section
	To begin	parallel ready		
1	turn west	L	twin knifehand guarding block	mid
2	step west	walking	inward knifehand strike	high
3	step east	L	knifehand guarding block	mid
4	step east	walking	flat finger-tip thrust	high
5	turn north	L	knifehand guarding block	mid
6	turn south	bending ready A		
7			right foot side piercing kick	mid
8	turn north	L	knifehand guarding block	mid
9	jump north		right flying side kick, double motion	
		L	knifehand guarding block	mid
10	turn east	L	outer forearm block	low
11	slip left foot	walking	hands up as to grab opponent's head	
12	kick upward with right knee while pulling both hands down			mid
13	turn west	walking	right reverse knifehand strike	high
14			right turning kick fast	high
15			left back piercing kick fast	mid
16	turn east	L	outer forearm block	mid
17			left turning kick (to N/E)	mid
18	turn south	fixed	U-shaped block	
19	jump	L	knifehand guarding block	mid
20	step south	walking	right upset finger tip thrust	low
21	pull left foot	L	right rear back fist strike	high
		L	left outer forearm block	low
22	step south	walking	right straight finger tip thrust	mid
23	turn west	walking	left double forearm block	high
24	step west	sitting	right outer forearm block	mid
		sitting	right rear back fist strike	high
25	kick east		right side piercing kick	mid
26	kick east		left side piercing kick	mid
27	turn west	L	cross knifehand side block	mid
28	step west	walking	twin upward palm hand block	mid
29	turn east	walking	right rising block	high
30		walking	reverse punch	mid
	To end	parallel ready	left foot moves	

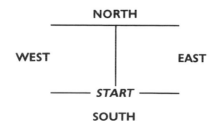

PATTERNS

ACKNOWLEDGEMENTS

A work of this kind is an exciting project, depending on support from many quarters.

Martin Hopper, Black Belt 2nd Dan and a fellow enthusiast for clarity and accuracy, is a long-standing friend (and opponent). His idea of presenting the patterns in the form of an easy-to-follow reference is a valuable contribution to the book.

Martin is one of the group of talented black belt models in the book, along with his daughter Jo (also a 2nd Dan) and Roger Lowther 1st Dan. Others generous with their help as models are Martin's elder daughter Louise and his wife Valerie; William and Clauda Webb, Nigel and Karen Hoskins, my daughters Jenny and Ruth, and Ruth's husband Adrian.

The very exacting work of photographing these models was carried out with painstaking patience by John Gichigi – he also doubled as a model (he is in his own right an accomplished martial artist).

In many parts of the country are experts, both ITF and WTF, too many to mention individually, who willingly responded to my requests for information and clarification on the finer points of the art of Taekwondo.

Finally, there are those who did not literally leap to my help in the physical sense but were ever willing in their support. So thanks to my wife Chris, and to my Mum and Dad.

USEFUL ADDRESSES

The British Taekwondo Council
58, Wiltshire Lane
Eastcote
Middlesex
HA5 2LU
Tel: 081 429 0878

The Amateur Martial Association
120, Cromer St
London
WCIH 8BS
Tel: 071 837 4406

The Martial Arts Commission
1st Floor
Broadway House
15/16 Deptford Broadway
London
SE8 4PA
Tel: 081 691 3433

The Sports Council
16, Upper Woburn Place
London
WCIH 0QP
Tel: 071 388 1277

The Taekwondo Association of Great Britain
6, Avon Road
Whitnash
Leamington Spa
CV31 2NJ
Tel: 0926 336322